MW00344184

IMAGES
of America

NORTHERN CALIFORNIA
DRAG RACING

ON THE COVER: In 1967 Fremont, California, Rich Guasco's nitro-powered pure hell bantam roadster blasts down the quarter-mile with Dale "the Snail" Emery at the controls. (Author's collection.)

IMAGES
of America

NORTHERN CALIFORNIA
DRAG RACING

Steve Reyes

ARCADIA
PUBLISHING

Copyright © 2021 by Steve Reyes
ISBN 978-1-4671-0817-1

Published by Arcadia Publishing
Charleston, South Carolina

Printed in the United States of America

Library of Congress Control Number: 2021953305

For all general information, please contact Arcadia Publishing:
Telephone 843-853-2070
Fax 843-853-0044
E-mail sales@arcadiapublishing.com
For customer service and orders:
Toll-Free 1-888-313-2665

Visit us on the Internet at www.arcadiapublishing.com

To my first grandchild, Obadiah Steven "Obi" Kelly.
Live your life to the fullest and be happy!

CONTENTS

Acknowledgments   6

Introduction   7

1.   "Lettuce" Entertain You:
   Racing at the Salad Bowl of the World   9

2.   Nitroholics: NorCal's Fast Guys   27

3.   The Funny Guys: The Sport Changes   71

4.   Little Guys: Backbone of the Sport   99

ACKNOWLEDGMENTS

Unless otherwise noted, all images appear courtesy of the author. Thanks to Mike Citro, Jamie and Sonny Jackson, Carl Olson, Frank Bradley, Bill Dunlap, Denny Forsberg, Richard Bruckman, Tom and Diane Walsh, and Gary Ritter for their information and insight that helped make this book possible. And for all those Northern California drag racers who blasted down the quarter-mile drag strips of "NorCal" from 1964 to 1973, a special thanks!

INTRODUCTION

Although the California hot rodding car culture believes that Southern California gave birth to the sport of organized drag racing, one could argue that Northern California had its own birth of the sport. The whole California hot rodding scene came alive after World War II. The returning GI's still needed and wanted excitement in their lives, and building hot rods proved to be a great outlet for those who had the "need for speed."

These hot rodders went out and about town and challenged each other to race on the city streets. This resulted in a dangerous atmosphere for those in the surrounding areas, as there were no real rules of engagement other than what those in attendance brought. There were also no safety considerations in where, when, and how they raced. In the interest of providing a safer place to race for both the racers and the spectators, car clubs were formed, and they petitioned local authorities to allow them to use abandoned airstrips that were scattered throughout Northern California.

Car clubs like the Hayward Headhunters approached city officials about using the abandoned airstrips to drag race. At first, they were turned down. However, after more than a few street races, it became paramount to city leaders and the police to curb the street racing. The clubs allied with the local police departments to work with the city officials to open the airstrips, providing racers with an outlet that was safer for all concerned.

During the 1950s, Salinas granted hot rodders a place to race at the Salinas Airport. It was not long before the California cities of Lodi (1951), Eureka (1951), Bakersfield (1952), Half Moon Bay (1953), Redding (1953), Vaca Valley (1956), Cotati (1956), and Fresno (1964) all followed suit. At Half Moon Bay, the airport was only a stone's throw from the Pacific Ocean, which was a beautiful backdrop for the racing.

As racing continued at the airstrips, it became obvious why they were airstrips and not drag strips. The runways had been built for airplanes, and they were not overly concerned with making sure that the runways were smooth and conducive to providing those racing with the maximum speed. Also, over time, they had developed bumps and imperfections that inhibited the car's ability to reach maximum speed without wreaking havoc. To allow the cars to run fast, it was imperative that a racetrack be designed to facilitate the racing in the safest manner. In 1959, a drag strip, not an airport, was opened in Fremont, California. It was a real drag strip that was built for racing. California's capital city of Sacramento welcomed the opening of its "built to race" drag strip as well. NorCal's wine country produced its own one-of-a-kind drag strip and road course in 1969. Sears Point, just outside of Vallejo, California, was state of the art for that time, incorporating new ideas to help racers run as fast as they could.

Of course, not all tracks were legal. NorCal outlaw tracks included Camp Stoleman in the Pittsburg/Antioch area. Then there was New Jerusalem in the Tracy area. The Winters track was located north of Vacaville, California. Oroville, California, also had its own outlaw drag strip, and finally there was Bonneville (San Jose). A track that only raced one year (1967) was in Vina, California.

Some of the biggest names in the sport of drag racing started out at these Northern California tracks. And some of the stars of the sport came from all over the United States to race at places like Bakersfield, Fremont, Sears Point, Half Moon Bay, Lodi, and Sacramento. Only a few of these racetracks still exist, but the memories of the tracks will last forever.

One

"LETTUCE"
ENTERTAIN YOU
RACING AT THE SALAD BOWL
OF THE WORLD

Before today's supermodern drag racing venues, there was racing on Southern California's dry lakes that took place in the 1930s. After World War II, there were many abandoned airstrips and runways in California where World War II pilots had trained. They came alive again with the sound of hot rodders racing. In the small farm town of Salinas, California, the city officials gave permission to promoter Red Jones to hold drag races at the local airport in 1949. Red Jones put on two drag racing events that were both a success, so he was offered the use of an unused auxiliary taxi runway next to the main airport for the following year. That was how organized drag racing in Northern California began.

In 1950, the Salinas Valley Timing Association organized and ran the racing at Salinas on that unused taxiway. The all-volunteer work staff made sure the racing ran smoothly from 1950 to 1970. It was a bare bones racetrack with no return road and no spectator side. When it got crowded in the holding area at the end of the track, racing stopped, and all the cars were brought back up the race surface and returned to the pit area. The spectator side had cows gazing lazily as the cars raced down the track. A gutted bread truck from the 1950s was the "tower" with the announcer calling the races. During the mid-1960s, a small wooden shed replaced the bread truck, giving the track a more modern look. The flag starter for the track was local racer Red Scardina. Red did his job well until 1968, when Salinas rented a Christmas tree starting system that replaced Red and his flag.

Since no one wanted any wayward race cars to venture onto any active runways, 55-gallon drums filled with sand lined the track as well as the very end of the taxiway. The track surface was not the smoothest or really level. In fact, the starting line had a slight incline. Dragster drivers had to hold the brake so the car would not just start rolling down the track while on the starting line.

It was crude, but Salinas was the place that started organized drag racing in Northern California. At one time, it was the oldest operating drag strip in the United States—not too bad for a place called "the salad bowl of the world."

The Salinas-based San Paolo brothers launched their top gas dragster down the well-used surface of the Salinas drag strip. This was in 1967, and the track had already seen 17 years of racing. The right side of the track is the so-called "spectator" side. The "spectators" were cows that would put their heads through the wire fence and graze through the racing action.

This view shows the main airport and its tower. Salinas's first airport was the Salinas American Legion Airport or Legion Field. It was only open from 1928 to 1933. It was then closed until it reopened in 1941 as Salinas Army Airfield during World War II. After the war, it became a fixture in the Salinas area for commercial and passenger flights. This is John Blount and his Wynns 1932 Ford "Spit Fire" coupe making a run down the track.

On the track in 1966 is San Jose, California–based Frankie Alves and his Dos Palmas–sponsored D/dragster. Also in this photograph is the Salinas bread truck "tower." Early on, when the track needed a place to put the announcer and timing equipment, this gutted-out bread truck fit the bill. The following year, the truck gave way to a newly built shed with windows and a locking door.

This battle between Salinas and San Jose took place in 1967. Local boy Rob Stirling (near side) and his Jack Stirling Automotive B/FD took on Terry Erven (far side) and his San Jose–based Goodies Speed Shop C/FD. Both of these cars ran on nitromethane and were fuel injected. Both were regular competitors at Salinas and other drag strips in NorCal. Stirling went on to the A/FD class and then, in the 1970s, raced in the top fuel dragster class. Erven parked his dragster and raced a nitro-burning blown fuel roadster called "Axis Power" from 1969 to 1970.

Making the tow from San Francisco was Frank Silva and the John Zoucha–owned, Gateway Chevrolet–sponsored top gas dragster. From 1965 to 1967, Silva was a fixture in top gas racing in the NorCal area. The blown Chevy gas burner was a fan favorite wherever it raced.

Blown gas altereds were a rare sight at Salinas. In 1967, when Ken Peterson brought his "Baby Huey" Fiat from the Bay area, it was a special treat for Salinas drag fans. His tire-smoking runs did not set any records, but the fans loved seeing Baby Huey do its thing.

This was in 1968 but it could have been 1950 with Phil Brooks and his Ford Flathead–powered "Bad News" roadster. Brooks's race car was a great example of what first raced down the Salinas taxiway in 1950 or even the Salinas Airport in 1949. In 1949, the city fathers of Salinas allowed Red Jones to have two races at the main airport, and the rest is history.

Sunnyvale's Gene Loflin raced one of the first "funny cars" at Salinas in 1967. Loflin's "the Greatest" Ford Falcon came to Salinas and made a few exhibition runs to the delight of Salinas drag fans. At the time, the funny car class, or A/FX class, was a new creation in drag racing. Seeing one of these cars in person was a real treat.

The first funny car to ever grace the Salinas taxiway was Joe Davis's "Colt .45" Mustang, based in San Jose. It was in 1966, when Davis had swapped his Fiat altered body for a Mustang body. He switched from gas to nitromethane in his engine and went to make money in the early funny car match racing circuit around the United States. His efforts in funny car racing proved to be a bust. Davis returned in a big way in the Davis and Ingram "Jewel T."

One of the few supercharged gas coupes that ran at Salinas belonged to Phil Nunez and Ed Dillon of Salinas. Their 1941 Willys pickup truck had a blown Chevy engine on pump gas. Larry Johnson was at the controls because the regular driver, Phil Nunez, was still recovering from a bad crash in their Willys coupe at Fremont in 1967.

In 1966, Carl Olson put laps on his newly purchased Plymouth-powered A/FD "the Hooligan." All drag racers looked for that winning edge when racing at all drag strips, and Olson was no different. Being a savvy and shrewd driver, he gathered information on flag starter Red Scardina. Olson learned Scardina feared nitro-burning race cars. When it was time to race, Olson staged his Hooligan and brought up the RPMs in his engine. Invariably, it spooked Scardina into pulling the starter flag, and Olson was off and running with a great start on the car he was running against.

A very rare car that was known to grace the Salinas 1,320 was a top fuel dragster. Stockton, California's Don Bowman was one of the few who tried out the Salinas track. This was in 1968 and Bowman's second top fuel car in two years. Don crashed his other top fuel car at the March Meet at Bakersfield, California. The only thing injured besides the car was his pride. He later loaned out his engine to Jim Nicoll, and his engine ended up being the runner-up car in Top Fuel Eliminator.

The future national champions went head-to-head at Salinas in 1967. By the end of 1967, Chico Breschini (near side) had collected B/dragster class at the NHRA Winternationals and was the Competition Eliminator champion. He went on to win Competition Eliminator at the NHRA World Finals, making him world champion in Competition Eliminator. Joe Davis (far side), in the Davis and Ingram Jewel T roadster, captured AA/A class honors at the NHRA US Nationals. When Davis won the Super Eliminator at the 1969 NHRA World Finals, he became world champion in Super Eliminator for that year.

Monterey-based Ace Bradford not only raced at Salinas, he was also the head of the Horsepower of Monterey Car Club. His Bradford Automotive was a place where any racer could seek help for repairs on their race car. Since Salinas only raced on the first Sunday of each month, Bradford could be found racing at Fremont or Half Moon Bay when Salinas was dark.

Ace Bradford debuted his Bantam-bodied altered in 1968 and ran it as well as his roadster body dragster. This style, Bantam, was very rare in drag racing. The open-style Bantam was used in the Altered classes but the Bantam with a roof not so much. The most well-known Bantam of this style body raced out of the Chicagoland area. It belonged to Gabby Bleeker, and it had nitro-burning blown Hemi in it.

Top gas guru Dick Oswald wrenched on one of his top gas dragsters at Salinas in 1968. The San Jose–based Oswald was a master engine builder and also helped many a driver procure much-needed seat time in his dragsters. Bill Dunlap, Dan Madigan, Dave Uyehara, and Frank Silva all had seat time in Oswald's top gas dragsters at one time.

The top gas team of Dick Oswald, Lee Cohen, and Dave Uyehara came together rather well in 1968. When the team raced at Salinas, they were the guys to beat. The team went on to race a top fuel dragster from 1970 to 1971 with Uyehara at the controls. Salinas businessman Lee Cohen was the manager of the Salinas drag strip for its last two years (1968–1970). Cohen made improvements, like bringing in a Christmas tree starting system. Unfortunately, it was not enough to save the track.

Another daring young man in his nitro-powered dragster was Frank Martinez. Martinez and his partner, Leroy Jorgensen, brought their top fuel dragster to run at Salinas. Martinez laid down a few nice safe runs that Sunday afternoon in 1968. Toward the end of 1968, Martinez and Jorgensen lost their race car at Fremont. A two-car crash totaled their car, but thankfully, Martinez walked away unhurt. The world's fastest Mexican returned in 1969 with a new partner in top fuel.

Top gas dragster driver Frank Silva became very familiar with the racing surface of Salinas. Over the span of four years (1966–1970), Silva drove four different top gas dragsters down the Salinas taxiway and took home quite a few Top Eliminator trophies.

San Jose's Arnold Chaves was another NHRA national champion who enjoyed Sunday afternoons at Salinas. He and his "Dos Palmas Machine" D/Altered won Competition Eliminator honors at the 1966 NHRA Winternationals at Pomona, California. Then he returned to the 1967 NHRA Winternationals to score a win in the D/Altered class. That year, Chaves also tried to compete in top gas with a new dragster. Finally, Chaves parked his Dos Palmas Machine to give his business the attention it needed to continue to thrive.

In 1968, the "Starvation" top gas dragster was hopelessly outdated. However, that did not stop the owners from racing the first Sunday of every month at Salinas. The Salinas-based drag team always put on a show for the fans with its smoking runs.

Rob Stirling debuted his all-new Ken Mitchell chassis A/FD in 1968. The Salinas resident and longtime racer parked his heavy, outdated B/FD for a sleek and slim A/FD. He was then able to do battle with the top gas dragster that invaded Salinas on a regular basis. Here, Stirling (near side) takes on Frank Silva driving the Arigoni and Grigg top gas dragster.

The funny car invasion of 1967 was led by Carter and Little's "Chevy II Heavy" blown nitro-burning Chevy Nova. Based out of Newark, California, this team raced all over California from 1967 to 1968. Ed Carter found the bite in the Salinas track to his liking. In the background of this photograph is the Schilling spice factory. If the wind was blowing the right way, the racetrack area smelled like the spice or spices being produced that day—no stinky exhaust fumes for Salinas.

The Lujan brothers raced one of the most unique dragsters to ever grace the Salinas quarter-mile. Their Salinas-based dragster was powered by a Lycoming four-cylinder airplane engine. The brothers were sponsored by Gold Coast Aviation of Salinas and were regulars at Salinas from 1967 to 1970.

Another new funny car that flexed its muscle at Salinas in 1967 was the all-new "Parts Mart" Camaro. The team of Snell, Von Uhlit, and Burnett came to Salinas from Campbell, California, to make a few test runs with their new injected nitro-burning Camaro. Kip Brundage was the driver and main sponsor. He was also the owner of the Parts Mart Speed Shop in Campbell, California. A little-known fact about this car is that it was built from the ground up by top fuel racer Frank Martinez, who had changed his mind and sold his newly built Camaro.

A NorCal fan favorite was the Souza Bros. and Dad Ford Mustang funny car. The Souza family was based in Hayward, California, and raced mainly in NorCal. "Big Dave" Souza was the driver, while brother Harold tuned the nitro-burning injected small-block Ford engine. Being one of the first funny cars in NorCal, the car had a modified chassis and a steel body. A fiberglass front clip and fiberglass doors were used to drop the weight. Funny cars were starting to use tube steel chassis and one-piece fiberglass bodies, which made the Souzas' Mustang very outdated even in 1967.

In 1968, the Souza Bros. and Dad returned to Salinas with a revamped Ford Mustang funny car. The car had been lengthened, and gone was the injected small-block engine. In its place was a big bad blown Ford wedge engine. Soon the blown wedge engine was replaced with a 427 Ford SOHC engine donated by Vic Hubbard Speed and Marine in Hayward, California.

Another Mustang funny car from the Bay Area was the Perry brothers' "Orion." The home-built race car was powered by a blown nitro-burning Pontiac engine. When the car was debuted in late 1966, Paul Perry was at the driver's controls. However, Perry had problems keeping the car straight, so longtime gas coupe owner and driver Steve Woods replaced Paul as the driver in 1967.

One of the big four NorCal funny cars that were sponsored by Goodies Speed Shop in San Jose was Don Williamson's "Hairy Canary," a blown Hemi-powered Plymouth Valiant. Out of all the Goodies-based funny cars, the Canary was the only one to come and race at Salinas in 1968. Don Williamson did the driving and tuning, and the car was based in San Jose.

After his 1966 funny car career went bust, Joe Davis went and partnered with Wes Ingram. It was then that the Jewel T AA/A was created in 1967. Salinas fans loved the bright-red and chromed roadster. In 1967, at the NHRA Division Seven points final, the Jewel T set the record for the AA/C and BB/GD classes. Since it already held the AA/A class record, the one car held three different class records at one time. This was possible by adding or subtracting weight from the race car and running against the existing record.

The top eliminator battle in 1967 was the Starvation top gas dragster (near side) versus the "Oswald and Dunlap" top gas dragster (far side). If this race had been in 1948, then the winner could have been greeted in the winner's circle by the Diamond Queen of Salinas, a young unknown starlet named Marilyn Monroe. When Salinas resident John Steinbeck based his book *East of Eden* on Salinas, he forgot to mention the drag races.

The class pairing of blower and gas versus injectors and nitro was frequent in early drag racing. The San Paolo brothers' top gas dragster (near side) took on Larry Johnson driving the Goodies-sponsored Lee's Automotive A/FD (far side) in 1967. The Salinas-based San Paolo team was extremely popular with fans and other racers. After every race at Salinas, the San Paolos welcomed all racers to their home for a giant spaghetti feed. They earned the team the nickname of the "Spaghetti Benders" among racers and race fans of Salinas.

The spectators (the cows) do not seem to be interested in the Davis and Ingram Jewel T. Just behind the photographer is a line of 55-gallon drums filled with sand. This ensured no wayward race cars would make it to the main runway of the Salinas airport. Salinas is one place a race car did not want a chute failure.

Two

NITROHOLICS
NorCal's Fast Guys

The King of the NorCal Quarter Mile was the nitro-gulping, front-engine, top fuel dragster, also known as the "slingshot"-style race car. These four-wheeled, 200-mile-per-hour, land-bound missiles were the main attraction at NorCal drag strips. From 1959 to 1971, these race cars were the fan favorite and quickest on the 1,320. At 300 feet per second, they were the fastest-accelerating race cars in the world. With rear slick tires churning smoke and front wheels dangling in the air, these cars put on a show like no other in any kind of motorsport. The best way to describe the men who piloted these nitro burners would be one word: fearless.

Fire, explosions, and hot oil baths were all in a day's racing for a top fuel dragster driver. Their need for speed outweighed the danger from participating in the sport. The real standout years for the front-engine top fuel class were from 1961 to 1971. In that decade, the front-engine top fuel dragster reached its peak in performance only to be replaced by the rear-engine top fuel dragster, which was introduced at the beginning of 1971.

For the hard-core top fuel fan, there will never be anything like watching a front-engine nitro-burning dragster running down the quarter-mile with a rooster tail of smoke and nitro flames belching from its exhaust pipes. Northern California had a great group of racers and race cars represented in drag racing's most exciting one-of-a-kind class. Unfortunately, when the design changed from front-engine to rear-engine, many Northern California race teams fell by the wayside. The new design only benefited a few of the Northern California top fuel racers.

Sacramento's Gary Ormsby adapted very well to the new design in top fuel racing. He went on to win 14 NHRA national events between 1984 and 1990. He was crowned the 1989 NHRA world champion in the top fuel class. Walnut Creek's carpet man Dennis Baca also stood out in national top fuel racing with two wins in 1977, the NHRA Nationals and NHRA World Finals. In March 1978, he took home top honors at the Bakersfield March Meet. Not to be outdone by Dennis Baca or Gary Ormsby, Napa's Frank Bradley collected big wins in NHRA top fuel competition. Bradley won the NHRA Winternationals in 1976, the 1984 NHRA Summernationals, the 1989 NHRA California Nationals, and the 1991 NHRA Winternationals.

Bay Area resident Dick Bertolucci owned and built the "Dolphin" dragster in 1954. The car was raced a short time in NorCal. But when Bertolucci's business took off, there was no time to drag race. For 30-plus years, the car sat in his shop before Bertolucci took it and restored it to its glory days.

State of the art in 1954 was the Sacramento-based "Glass Slipper" dragster of Ed and Roy Cortopassi and Doug Butler. It was the first dragster to combine a streamlined fiberglass body, aluminum frame, and enclosed canopy around the driver. It was a true one-of-a-kind race car for the mid-1950s.

In 1964, "Terrible Tempered" Ted Gotelli's South San Francisco–based top fuel dragster collected 17 top eliminator wins with three different drivers: Denny Miliani, Pete Ogden, and "Slammin' Sammy" Hale. Gotelli's car had a Kent Fuller chassis with a Gotelli-built 392 Chrysler Hemi.

John "the Sultan" Batto drove the first Woody Gilmore–built–chassis top fuel car in Northern California. The Batto, Valente, and Bings top fuel car was based in Santa Rosa, California. In 1965, the team ran an unheard-of 7.69 at 213 miles per hour at Fremont and was the rival of the Gotelli and Miliani team from South San Francisco. In 1965, both teams racked up five top eliminator wins at Fremont by June. Gotelli and Miliani broke the tie on July 11, 1965. It was their last win at Fremont, because Miliani died in a crash at Half Moon Bay on August 22, 1965.

Sam and Fred Bailey raced one of the few Drag Master chassis dragsters in Northern California. Racing out of their Napa, California, speed shop, the Bailey brothers had an unknown plumber/welder, Frank Bradley, at the controls of their injected Chevy fuel car. The Drag Master chassis had been an immensely popular dragster at the beginning of the 1960s. It was a "kit car" supplied by Dode Martin and Jim Nelson from Southern California.

The hard-running blown Chevy dragster of Bauer, Blessing, and Swansboro first appeared in early 1965. The team soon changed to become Braudrick, Bauer, and Blessing, and driver Danny Brown was replaced by Frank Bradley. The blown fuel Chevy ran well against NorCal's big bad blown fuel Hemi dragsters.

On August 22, 1965, Denny Miliani died at Half Moon Bay in the Gotelli and Miliani top fuel dragster. A chute failure on a 207-mile-per-hour pass caused the car to leave the racing surface and flip in the shutdown area. Sadly, this was not the first driver Ted Gotelli lost in a racing accident. On September 10, 1962, Glen Leasher was killed driving Romeo Palamides's "Infinity" F86-powered jet race car at Bonneville. That same year, Leasher had driven Gotelli's car to a runner-up spot at Bakersfield against Don Prudhomme.

San Leandro, California–based Nick Mura raced his Fuller chassis Plymouth Wedge fuel car when he was not attending to his wholesale nursery business. In 1963 and 1964, the car ran a blower on its Plymouth Stage III Wedge head V-8 on nitro. The driver was Denny Miliani, and he drove Mura's car when his regular ride in Ted Gotelli's fuel car was parked or he was arguing with "Terrible Ted." During this time, a young coast guardsman named Carl Olson was crewing for Mura and Miliani.

Old race cars found new life in Northern California. Tony Waters's 1959 fuel roadster found new life as the Matelli and Perkins fuel roadster in 1965. The San Francisco–based team only raced the roadster a few times, because it was hopelessly outdated. The car was retired, and in 1966, Jessie Perkins debuted "the Runt" top fuel dragster, with Rich Bruckman at the controls. Bruckman at one time snuck into the drags in a friend's car trunk because he had no admission money, and then he was driving one of the quickest and fastest cars on the quarter-mile.

Running out of George Santos S&S Automotive in Hayward, California, was the nitro-burning injected Chevy "Gold Finger" fuel dragster. Owned and tuned by Santos and driven by Jim Perry, this injected Chevy fuel car ran well enough to put the big bad Hemi-powered boys on the trailer in top eliminator wars during 1965 and 1966.

Early in 1965, the team of Hay, Haslam, and Walsh debuted their top fuel dragster "the Wailer." Soon after, the team became John "Lefty" Hay and Tom Walsh with Walsh driving as Haslam had left the team. From 1965 to 1970, the Wailer toured NorCal, "SoCal," and Canada and raced in Hawaii. Over those five years and two Wailer race cars, the team had as drivers Tom Walsh, Frank Martinez, Rich Zoucha, Dale Emery, Bill Alexander, and Wayne King.

Baumgardner, Trefethen, and Pearson raced as "the Whiz Kids" in the mid-1960s. Their driver, Walt Baumgardner, drove the top fuel car to relax from his real job as a USAF fighter pilot. Walt went to Vietnam for Uncle Sam, and Tommy Fults took over the driving chores for Baumgardner. Thankfully, Baumgardner was able to return home from Vietnam after his duty was over.

The second "Woody" car in NorCal was raced by Denny Forsberg and sponsored by Vic Hubbard Speed and Marine in Hayward, California. This nitro-burning Chevy-powered dragster raced in top fuel against the big bad blown top fuel cars of 1965 and 1966. Tuned by Jerry Light, this injected Chevy was a major player in top eliminator wherever it raced in NorCal.

The battle of speed shops in 1966 included Bings Speed Shop and Vic Hubbard's Speed and Marine, both with a nitro-burning injected Chevy. Bings's counterman Gene Gilmore drove the Santa Rosa–based dragster (near side), while Denny Forsberg was at the controls of the Hayward-based Hubbard's fuel dragster (far side). Both racers could be found in top eliminator and top fuel eliminator at NorCal drag strips throughout the mid- to late 1960s.

San Francisco's Chuck Flores believed in recycling before it was the "in" thing to do. This was Flores's second slightly used top fuel dragster. He first purchased Rich Guasco's top fuel dragster in 1964, and in 1966, he purchased the well-known Sour Sisters shark top fuel dragster. Chuck raced his "Shark" for four years until building a new dragster in 1970.

A pair of San Jose–based top fuel dragsters went head-to-head at Fremont in 1966. Davidson, Pike, and Silvera, with Ron Davidson driving, was on the near side, while Tom Prufer's "Power King II," with Gerry Steiner driving, was on the far side. The DPS dragster was the only nitro-burning 354 Desoto Hemi-powered car racing in top fuel in NorCal. The 392 Chrysler Hemi was the norm in NorCal and SoCal top fuel racing.

Frank Bradley's new ride in 1966 was the Bradley, Jorgensen, and Braudrick top fuel dragster. With Leroy Jorgensen tuning the Hemi for power, the team started to rack up victories in top eliminator all over NorCal. Bradley became drag racing's quickest and fastest plumber/welder.

One of the more successful top fuel teams in 1966 and 1967 was the team of, from left to right, Frank Bradley, Leroy Jorgensen, and Dick Braudrick. Drag racing was a part-time thing for this trio, as Bradley was a plumber/welder, Jorgensen owned a transmission repair shop, and Braudrick was the general manager of a cement company. Like most racers in NorCal, these guys worked for a living, and drag racing was a hobby.

The Concord, California–based Galli brothers were a regular fixture at NorCal racetracks for over a decade. There were three Galli brothers: Rich, Jimmie, and Oscar. Richard and Jimmie were the drag racers, starting out with a nitro-burning Olds. Then, in 1965, they switched to a 392 Hemi. Of course, Rich and Jimmie were working guys during the week, as both worked at Lehmer Chevrolet in Concord. There, Rich was a painter, and Jimmie was a body man.

Jim Davis was a race car builder, driver, and innovator in top fuel racing. It was 1966 when Davis pieced together a starter system for top fuel engines made from old airplane starters. With the help of craftsman Mike Citro, Davis successfully developed the top fuel starter system. Davis designed the special parts to be made, and Citro hand-made those parts. Davis did a pretty good business selling his starter kits and then sold the design to Childs and Albert in SoCal.

Wine country's Jimmy Haire was on his way to drag racing stardom in NorCal. He had just purchased a brand new "Woody" car for top fuel racing. But alas, Haire never reached stardom. Jimmy's dad gave him an ultimatum: drag racing or his inheritance of vineyards and huge amounts of farmland. Haire sold his Woody, which had only eight runs on it, and went for his inheritance.

Another cornerstone of NorCal top fuel racing was the San Leandro–based team of Sid Masters and Rich Richter. From 1961 to 1966, they were a staple of top fuel racing in NorCal. Bob Smith, Gerry Card, Bob Haines, Don LaBlount, Denny Miliani, Jim Herbert, Chuck Poole, and Russ Lewis all had driving time in the five years they raced in top fuel. In those five years, M&R became Ted Gotelli's biggest rival in NorCal top fuel racing, and it ended when M&R quit in 1967.

Do-it-yourselfer and ex-top gas racer Roger "Bone" Harrington was never one to set records with his plain blue Davis chassis top fuel dragster. The Richmond, California–based racer built his own engines and tuned them. He even painted his own race car. From 1964 to 1970, Harrington could be found racing at all NorCal drag strips. Most times, he arrived at the races with a new crew. Blower builder and friend Mike Citro lent a hand when he was not racing as well as local top gas racer Johnny Austin.

Roy and Marilyn Dunn were a husband-and-wife team out of Marysville, California. They started in top fuel with a blown Chevrolet on nitro. The dynamic duo switched to a 392 Hemi in 1966, which Roy drove and tuned, and Marilyn maintained the car by mixing fuel and packing the parachute. Wherever there was a top fuel event in NorCal, the Dunns were there between 1965 and 1969.

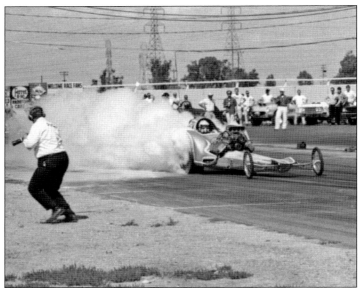

Coming off the car show circuit was the "Bushwacker" of Don Tognotti. Marc Danekas purchased the stunning show dragster and put it on the drag strip with Jack Martin at the controls. The one-of-a-kind body on the car proved to be too heavy. After the 1966 season, the car ended up parked in Danekas's Hayward, California, shop.

A head-to-head top fuel match between Ted Lemond's "the Spoiler" and "the Wailer" was also a match between Sacramento and Hayward, California. The Spoiler was near side with Bob Hall driving, and the Wailer was on the far side with Tommy Walsh driving. The flagman, Mike Mahay, was in the middle of these two nitro burners. Fremont had not yet switched to the Christmas tree starting system, so Mahay was starting the competition at the track this day in 1966.

Sporting his blonde Beatles wig was top fuel driver Bob Hall. In 1966, the Beatles had invaded the United States, so Hall wanted to show his support for the Fab Four. Hall was driving Ted Lemond's Spoiler, which was the former Capitol Speed Shop top fuel car based in Sacramento, California. Not only did Lemond own a top fuel dragster, but he also promoted top fuel races at Sacramento Raceway.

With jet dragster owner and builder Romeo Palamides based at the airport in Oakland, track manager Ron Lawrence booked many a top fuel dragster versus jet dragster match race at Fremont. Here, on a cool October 1966 evening, "the Untouchable" jet, with J.D. Zink driving, took on the Waters and Edmunds top fuel dragster, with John "the Black Knight" Edmunds driving. Race fans were treated to one heck of an incredible show of sound and fire.

There is nothing like a top fuel dragster at night. The flames, smoke, and sound were a one-of-a-kind treat for the spectators. On this night, the Zoucha, Stokes, and Jordan top fuel dragster put on a show with Rich Zoucha at the controls. The team was based in Hayward, California, and was a regular at top fuel races in NorCal during the 1966 and 1967 race seasons.

It was NorCal versus SoCal at Half Moon Bay sometime in 1966. Kenny Safford was driving Ted Gotelli's new "Woody" chassis top fuel dragster (near side) against Mike Snively driving Roland Leong's "Hawaiian" top fuel dragster (far side). This event marked the return of Ted Gotelli a year after the death of his driver Denny Miliani at Half Moon Bay. The SoCal-based Hawaiian won this match up with the then-new team of Gotelli and Safford.

The new top fuel team of Gotelli and Safford went anywhere and everywhere in California to race. Here, Gotelli and Safford (near side) faced off with the famed "Surfers" top fuel dragster (far side) of Skinner, Jobe, and Sorokin at the *Hot Rod* magazine championships held in Riverside, California, in 1966. Surfers' driver, Mike Sorokin, put a holeshot on Gotelli and Safford, making them a first-round loser. The irony of this win was that the year before, Sorokin did the same to Gotelli and Miliani at the same race.

Walnut Creek resident Jim Davis became a major player in top fuel eliminator from 1965 to 1971. Davis was an innovator, chassis builder, driver, engine builder, tuner, and family man. His racing career may have never happened if it was not for his wife, Carol. In the early 1960s, Davis had a horrific top fuel dragster crash. The accident left Davis with a broken neck, an injury that had proved fatal for many people. Carol nursed her husband back from death's door. After a year or so, Davis was able to climb back into a top fuel dragster and race.

The Ace Head Shop top fuel dragster was unique because it was the only one with a nitro-burning blown big-block Pontiac engine. Naval reservist Larry Neumeyer drove the Pontiac-powered fuel car. In 1967, at Fremont, the Pontiac engine exploded in a ball of fire. Larry was burned on his hands and neck but managed to get the car stopped. Lying in a hospital bed, he worried not about his burns but whether or not the Navy would find out about his hobby. They did not take kindly to anyone damaging Navy property, and he was considered that property.

Bob and Don Berry went top fuel racing after running a fuel-burning roadster in 1964 and a junior fuel dragster with Rance McDaniel in 1965 and 1966. Their driver was Claude "the Wasp" Stark. The Selma, California–based team had Stark drive the 1967 season. Then John "Black Knight" Edmunds and Butch Maas saw seat time in 1968. After Maas, the Berry brothers went with Dwight Hughes as their driver from 1969 well into the 1970s.

From the age of 13, San Francisco's Richard Bruckman dreamed of driving a race car. When he was old enough, he built a 1929 Roadster with a nitro-burning flathead. The Roadster was not fast enough for Bruckman, so he procured a 130-mile-per-hour gas dragster. A pair of Willys gassers followed, but his big break came driving the Perkins and Matelli fuel roadster. Perkins liked his driving, so he ended up in the Perkins Runt fuel dragster in 1966. Then, in 1967, he piloted the "Perkins Cow Palace Shell" top fuel car.

Don Cook was the guy from Missouri who settled in Walnut Creek, California. In 1965, Cook partnered with Dwight Bale and ran a top fuel dragster. By 1966, Bale was gone, and Cook was partnered with Jim Nicoll and his Der Wienerschnitzel top fuel car "Top Dog." Then, in 1967, Cook was flying solo with his own Southwind top fuel car. Cook and his German shepherd Keno headed east and won the AHRA Nationals in New York. Cook toured for the next five years on the AHRA circuit as a top fuel pro.

"The Vagabond" top fuel car was named after a bar in Sacramento. Apparently, the co-owners frequented the bar and told the bar owner all about their racing glory. He enjoyed the stories so much he purchased a third of the car as long as the car was named after the bar. Gary Ormsby was not the original driver. Larry Leventon drove the car first, but when Leventon did not show up one day to drive the car, Ormsby borrowed a helmet and fire suit, climbed in the car, and ran 180 miles per hour in his first-ever run.

Gerry Card's Quicksilver fuel coupe was a crowd favorite in NorCal. Card's coupe was not a top fuel dragster, but it was not a fuel roadster either. It was kind of a top fuel car with a full body. Based in El Cerrito, California, it was housed at Gerry's Corvair service center. An interesting note was that before Card built his coupe, he drove both Masters and Richter's and Ted Gotelli's fuel cars in 1961.

Out of Clarksburg, California, Jim Brandy named his Chevy fuel car "Giant Killer" for a good reason. It slayed the blown Hemi cars on the quarter-mile. Brandy's lightning reflexes and the performance of his injected Chevy dragster sent many a blown dragster home. This photograph is a 1967 battle with Roger Harrington's blown nitro-burning Hemi (near side). Brandy outran the Hemi car on that long-ago day at Fremont.

During the 1960s and 1970s, it seemed like there was not a time when Sacramento's Jim Herbert was not driving a race car that did not run on nitromethane. He drove both fuel roadsters and top fuel dragsters for over a decade and did it very well. Pictured here is the Bishop, Pitts, and Herbert "Lizard" top fuel dragster from 1967. The team raced three different Lizards between 1966 and 1968.

Tommy Walsh (left) and John "Lefty" Hay (right) debuted the all-new Wailer in 1967. In the driver's seat was Frank Martinez, and it was his debut in a top fuel dragster. The new Wailer featured a Lefty Hay chassis and custom paint by Tony Del Rio. The engine was tuned and built by Walsh and Hay at their Hayward, California, shop.

In 1967, the Vic Hubbard gang tried something different in NorCal fuel racing: they built an injected Ford SOHC engine in top fuel. Driver Denny Forsberg only got to drive it about eight times before engine woes sidelined the car. The biggest problem the team had was the cost to replace broken or worn parts in the engine. The engine was pulled out of the dragster and sold to the Souza brothers for their Mustang funny car.

NorCal's Jeff Starr not only raced a top fuel dragster for a couple of seasons in the 1960s, but he was also NorCal's connection to the music and TV industry in SoCal. His sister Phyllis Jean was married to Mickey Jones, the drummer for Bob Dylan and founding member of Kenny Rogers's First Edition band. He played the drums on 17 gold records and appeared as a character actor in over two dozen TV sitcoms. The two biggest roles were in Tim Allen's *Home Improvement* and *Justified*.

Everybody loves a parade, right? Race fans at Kingdon Raceway in Lodi, California, enjoy this top fuel parade in 1967. Leading the parade was Roland Leong's Hawaiian, then Tom Hoover, and third in line, from Largo, Florida, was "Starvin' Marvin" Schwartz. Before Fremont opened in 1959, Kingdon was the place to race. Even toward the mid- to late 1960s, Kingdon still attracted the top fuel stars of drag racing.

Frank Pitts's top fuel driving career began in 1968 when he bought out his partners in the Lizard and went top fuel racing. At Bakersfield, Pitts was going to make his mark in top fuel racing, but it turned out to be the wrong kind of mark. While push-starting his race car, he lost control on the fire-up road and tangled with the spectator fence. The only thing hurt was Frank's wallet and, of course, the race car.

The helmet visor says it all. Denny Ball raced in top fuel from 1965 to 1969. His car had a Jim Davis chassis with a home-built 392 Chrysler Hemi. The Bay Area resident raced mainly at Fremont and Lodi. A few drivers that had raced Ball said he had this habit of climbing out of his car after a run and vomiting. Then he climbed back in his car and was pushed back into his pit area.

The San Jose, California, race team of Jon Halstead and Bill Dunlap were well-known top gas dragster racers in NorCal in 1967. The following year, it was time to go top fuel racing with a 427 Ford SOHC engine in their dragster. Both a Chrysler Hemi and the Ford saw time in their dragster during the 1968 season. The duo decided to leave the Ford behind and stay with the 392 Chrysler Hemi for 1968 and 1969.

In 1968, Noel Black built a rather strange twin-engine dragster, with one engine in front of the driver and one hung out over the front wheels. Black called his creation "the Rhinoceros," and it ran on nitro. Noel's NorCal business was B&N Automotive, where he built chassis and components for race cars. After testing, the Rhino was fitted with a streamliner body and headed to the Bonneville Salt Flats. In 1970, at Bonneville, while running over 300 miles per hour, a tire failure simultaneously destroyed the Rhino and killed Black.

That kid from Oklahoma got himself one heck of a top fuel dragster ride. Late in 1967, Gary Ormsby found himself at the controls of the Cameron, Naify, and Rapadas brothers "Cheetah" top fuel dragster. Living in Sacramento, Ormsby worked at a Sacramento car dealership fetching parts while on roller skates and then he had a full-time top fuel ride. The Cheetah was a recycled race car that had been owned by Bob Sbarboro and raced in 1965–1966.

It was almost the end of the line for the Walsh and Hay Wailer and the Jorgensen and Martinez top fuel dragster in 1968. Rich Zoucha was driving the Wailer and received an oil bath at the finish line, making it impossible to see. He ran over the front of the Jorgensen and Martinez fuel car, and the ensuing crash destroyed both cars. Thankfully, both drivers walked away. The Wailer was rebuilt in a week with Frank Martinez back in the driver's seat.

In Fresno, California, James Warren was sure that he was never going to rust while driving the Warren, Coburn, and Miller top fuel dragster. Hot oil is being pumped onto the driver at 200 miles per hour. That was just one of many hazards a driver could encounter while driving a top fuel dragster in 1968. Warren got stopped okay, but he was a bit oily.

It was a scary time for Jim Davis as his top fuel dragster left the racing surface at 180-plus miles per hour. Davis went off-roading at Fresno in 1968. He finally gained control and was able to bring his wayward car back onto the track. Davis just missed the photographer, who was up against the inside of the eight-foot chain-link fence.

The husband-and-wife team of Walt and Debbie Anderson owned the show-and-go Eastside Kids top fuel Chevy-powered dragster. To be honest, the Andersons' car was more show than go. However, when it was at the racetrack, J.D. Zink or Don Clar both took turns behind the steering wheel in 1968. Here, the car is at Lions Drag Strip in Long Beach, California, competing at the Professional Dragsters Association race in 1968.

The one thing a top fuel dragster driver fears is fire. In 1968, Jim Hebert's fears came true while driving the Lizard top fuel dragster. Hebert received second- and third-degree burns on his hands when an oil bath erupted into a very hot burning fire. Herbert had no choice but to ride out the fire; it was so hot it cooked Jim's hands in his gloves. Of course, he was back soon after with bandages and new Nomex-lined gloves. Not even painful burns can sideline a top fuel driver.

James Warren, in the Warren, Coburn, and Miller top fuel dragster, took home top fuel honors at the 1968 NHRA Winternationals in Pomona, California. This was the trio's first big win at an NHRA National event, and it was not their last. Warren with Roger Coburn had won top gas eliminator at the Smoker's March Meet at Bakersfield in 1960 for their first "big race win."

Sacramento's Larry "Shorty" Leventon was the supreme journeyman top fuel dragster driver. From all reports, he started driving Greg Maher's dragster in 1961. His driving saga would continue in Bob Sbarboro's "Renegade" and "Cheetah," "the Vagabond," Wolf and Maher, B&N Automotive, Wulf and Loy, Wulf and Semus, and of course, his own top fuel dragsters during the 1970s.

Don Argee was known as the "Don" of the Sacramento racing "mafia." A longtime drag racer, Argee was well known in 1965 as the driver of the Brocchini and Argee fuel-burning roadster. The roadster held the standard 1,320 record at 9.358 seconds at 164.88 miles per hour. Argee was a cement-truck driver by trade who was also a top fuel driver/owner and the president of the Sacramento UDRA chapter. To relax, he sometimes could be found driving Fred Sorensen's fuel altered.

Fresno businessman and top fuel boat racer Ed Wills went top fuel dragster racing in the late 1960s with Dan Olson as his crew chief and a Paul Gommi–built Hemi in an RCS chassis. Stan Shiroma and then Vic Brown drove the Fresno-based top fuel dragster. In the early 1970s, Wills raced both a rear-engine top fuel car and a funny car. Jack Martin drove the dragster, and the funny car had Kelly Brown, Dave Beebe, Mike Snively, and Bobby Rowe as drivers.

Wayne "the Peregrine" King was a fixture in NorCal and SoCal top fuel racing during the 1960s. Doss, Clayton, and King; Donovan Engineering; Tony Waters; Crossley and King; and the Wailer are a few of the top fuel dragsters that the Peregrine drove. His nickname came about in the mid-1960s, when top fuel drivers were adopting animal or bird names. "The Mongoose," "the Snake," "the Eagle," and "the Mandrill" were just a few others used by drivers of top fuel dragsters.

Gary Ritter and Willie Kinner appeared on the NorCal top fuel scene toward the end of the 1960s. The Hayward, California–based duo purchased a Jim Davis–built dragster, and Willie Kinner supplied the 392 Hemi built by him in his Hayward engine shop. On Ritter's final run to get his NHRA top fuel license, he had a massive blower explosion. The backplate on the blower hit Ritter in the head, knocking him out. He did manage to pull the chute and stop the car. It was old-style top fuel racing at its best.

Boston-born Mike Citro headed for NorCal in 1963 and set up shop in the Walnut Creek area. His skills as a tool and die maker were put to good use in the mid-1960s by Jim Davis, Don Cook, Dennis Baca, and Dwight Bale. He made custom parts and pieces for many racers in NorCal. From 1968 to 1970, Citro went top fuel racing with the help of Davis. With the costs rising in top fuel racing, Mike switched to racing an injected fuel car. His good friends the Galli brothers helped set up his new car.

Doug Timmons was at his Chico-based shop readying the car for its debut on New Year's Day 1967 at Lodi, California. He had a big problem on New Year's Eve as he climbed in his car and fired it up in front of his shop. He drove down the street and turned around. As he headed toward the shop, he discovered the car had no brakes. The car sideswiped his new Chevy truck and then ran across the street into a cyclone fence. He did not make the race the next day.

Walnut Creek's Dennis Baca started out in a blown fuel flat-bottom boat then went land drag racing with Dwight Bale in 1965. Soon, Baca purchased a Jim Davis car, and a long successful top fuel career that spanned over three decades took off. This is Baca's last front-engine top fuel car with partner Larry Freels in 1970. Baca was one of the first California top fuel racers to switch to a rear-engine top fuel dragster in late 1971.

Dwight Bale was a wandering top fuel gypsy. In the early to mid-1960s, he and his wife, Helga, toured the country with his top fuel dragster before settling in Walnut Creek, California, in 1963. Bale and good friend Jim Davis went urban white water rafting down the Walnut Creek aqueduct in February 1973. The raft overturned, and Bale drowned at only 30 years of age. The ironic thing about Bale's death was that he also drove the blown fuel hydro "Conquest" but died while trying to navigate a small craft.

This was another 1970 winner's circle for Dennis Baca and friends. Standing from left to right are crew chief Gary Walters, pal Kenny Safford, Bob Sbarboro, Anna Baca, Dennis Baca, Terry Baca, and Bradley and Brent Davis. Gary Walters, who owned Stockton Engine and Machine in Stockton, California, wrenched for Baca, Don Cook, and Jim Davis.

A NorCal top fuel metamorphosis occurred when Zoucha, Stokes, and Jordan became the "El Lobo" of Zoucha and Jordan. Then the El Lobo became "the Californian" of Zoucha, George Stokes, Larry Jordan, Jerry Stokes, and Bob Pollard. That happened over a three-year period between 1966 and 1969. Zoucha drove all the cars except one weekend when SoCal's Hugh "Putzel" Osterman drove the Californian at Sacramento.

Sacramento's Kenny Machost looks for the finish line in the sky at Fremont in 1970. Early in his career, Machost replaced Gary Ormsby in the Vagabond. Kenny then had a string of top fuel dragster rides, and "the Sky Pilot" fuel car was his own race car. Note the weight bar that he has just run over bouncing behind the car.

The NorCal team of Dick Oswald, Lee Cohen, and Dave Uyehara switched from gasoline to nitro in 1970. The trio raced in NHRA Division 7 and followed the series all over California and Salt Lake City, Utah, in pursuit of championship points. Besides driving a race car, Uyehara also built race car chassis for a living. His business was good, so US touring with a race car was not practical for him.

Arnold Birky and Bob Neal were very well-known junior fuel racers in NorCal. Their red dragster with a nitro-burning injected Chevy engine raced all over NorCal in the mid- to late 1960s. However, 1970 saw big changes for the Napa/Sonoma-based duo. Gone was their injected nitro-burning Chevy-powered dragster. In its place was an all-new blown 392 Hemi nitro burner for Bob "the Worm" Neal to drive and Arnold Birky to tune.

Owning a top fuel dragster was a dream come true for wheelchair-bound Bill Wishart. Early in 1970, his dream debuted with Wild Bill Alexander driving and Bob Sbarboro building and tuning the 392 Hemi. Veteran chassis builder Pete Ogden helped Wishart achieve his goal with a sleek new chassis. Wishart's Fremont-based fuel car was featured in *Hot Rod* magazine, and it toured NorCal and SoCal drag strips from 1970 to 1971.

That was raw fuel being pumped onto driver Johnny Cox's face as the Welty, Smith, and Cox "Cheetah II" exploded a blower at Fresno in 1971. Cox was not injured, but the blower sure was. The Cheetah II was a team car to the Cameron, Naify, and Rapadas brothers Cheetah. The No. 2 Cheetah was also the longest front-engine top fuel car in NorCal at 200 inches.

On July 11, 1970, Bill Dunlap was driving the Blanchard and Dunlap top fuel car when a rear tire exploded just before the finish line at Lions Drag Strip in Southern California. The explosion blew off the cowl and knocked out Dunlap. The car crossed over the left lane into the guardrail, destroying the car. Dunlap sustained a broken rib and a shrapnel wound in his left leg. The NorCal duo returned to racing in a different car.

Redding, California–based Dennis Hollingsworth owned one of the few full-bodied top fuel dragsters in NorCal. Longtime racer and competitive water skier Jerry Vargas was the driver for Hollingsworth's "Dennis the Menace" fuel car. The duo raced in top fuel from 1967 to 1970 before Hollingsworth retired and moved to Southern California. Vargas continued with his water-skiing competition.

The NorCal team of Don Durbin and Bob Nestor only raced together for a short time in the early 1970s. Nestor bowed out, and Durbin continued to race until the car was obsolete. Durbin was an electrician by trade, so he put a little spark into his racing by building a brand-new rear-engine top fuel car. He named it "My Favorite Thing (almost)." Durbin and his top fuel car toured the United States in the 1970s and 1980s.

Diehard Gerry Steiner did not let go of his front-engine top fuel dragster. He raced it well into 1972, when the rear-engine dragster had already taken over the title of King of the Quarter Mile. About 20 years after he parked his beloved front-motor fuel car, the retro top fuel class began in nostalgia drag racing in the 1990s. There was Steiner again, wheeling a new front-engine top fuel car in competition.

This was the last run for the Olson and Bowman top fuel car in 1971. SoCal's Carl Olson drove, and NorCal's Don Bowman wrenched their top fuel car. On this run, Olson received a hot oil bath at the finish line. He pulled his chute, but since he could not see, he veered off the track. The car struck the lip of the first turnout road and flipped, destroying the car. Olson continued to race in top fuel with Mike Kuhl, and Don Bowman went racing with Marc Danekas and Ron Banks.

At top fuel car and boat racer Dwight Bale's funeral in 1973, a group of racer friends thought of a great send-off for their fallen comrade. They transported his coffin in a blown fuel hydro boat modified to hold the coffin instead of a hearse, and away it went to the gravesite. When the coffin was lowered into the grave, Tommy Fults and Ron Campagnoli fired up the boat and racked the throttle. Waking up the dead had a new meaning that day.

Heading for the moon at Lions Drag Strip was Dwight Hughes and the Berry brothers' top fuel dragster. It was 1971, and soon after, the Selma, California–based team made the move into the rear-engine top fuel dragster movement. Brother Don Berry only raced a few more seasons in top fuel, and then he switched to a World of Outlaws sprint car with Chuck Miller driving. Bob Berry and Dwight Hughes then retired from racing.

One of two top fuel rides for Dave Uyehara in 1971 was Max Williams's "Instant Karma," and the other was the "Gold Seeker" top fuel dragster. With his Karma ride in NorCal and his Seeker ride in SoCal, Uyehara put on a few miles driving on California Highway 99 between San Jose and Los Angeles. Max Williams hired journeyman driver Denver Schutz to drive when Uyehara could not make the drive back to NorCal.

Coming out of the Sacramento area was John Shoemaker and his top fuel dragster. Shoemaker was a true craftsman, building race car chassis and race car components. Many a race car had a Shoemaker chassis in top fuel. His customers included Don Turner and Bill and Claire Stammerjohan, and for his last front-engine fuel car, Gary Ormsby chose a Shoemaker chassis.

The small NorCal town of Turlock, California, at one time had three top fuel dragster teams. The team of father Earl and son Rich Heidt raced a home-built top fuel car. Building his own top fuel dragster was Howard Sweet, a Turlock resident (pictured). Finally, the husband-and-wife team of Bill and Claire Stammerjohan raced a Shoemaker chassis top fuel car in the closing days of the front-engine top fuel dragster in drag racing around 1972.

Even in 1967, drag racers recycled, and NorCal's Jim Lind was that kind of guy. Lind purchased the former "Magicar" of Winkel, Trapp, and Glenn based out of SoCal. He converted it to his "Uptight, Out of Sight" top fuel dragster. The car underwent changes like lengthening the chassis and removing the full body. Lind ran the car for a few seasons then parked it.

Gary Ormsby's last front-engine top fuel car was a John Shoemaker car. Ormsby began in 1972 with his then-outdated top fuel dragster, but soon after this event in early 1972, he and George Wulf teamed up and raced an all-new rear-engine top fuel dragster. It took 17 years of hard racing, but in 1989, Ormsby became the NHRA world champion in Top Fuel Eliminator—the only NorCal top fuel racer to ever achieve this goal up to that date.

This was the future of top fuel racing starting in 1971. Florida's Don Garlits made the rear-engine concept work, so others soon followed suit. The first to have a rear-engine top fuel dragster racing out of NorCal was Dennis Baca. Based in Walnut Creek, Baca was one of four NorCal top fuel racers who did very well in a rear-engine top fuel car. Gary Ormsby, Frank Bradley, and James Warren all posted national event victories for Northern California.

Three

THE FUNNY GUYS
THE SPORT CHANGES

Since the beginning of drag racing, innovation has been a large part of the sport. Less than 20 years after the first organized drag race, a major innovation changed the sport forever. In 1964, former top fuel dragster owner/driver Jack Chrisman and the SoCal auto dealership of Sachs and Sons debuted a race car that turned the sport upside down. No, it was not a dragster, but a stock-bodied new 1964 Mercury Comet with a blown nitro-burning engine and dragster-style slick tires in the rear. Utilizing a high-gear-only transmission to get the power to the rear slicks, Chrisman and the Comet hit the 1,320 with incredible tire-smoking quarter-mile runs to the delight of the fans in the grandstands. Because there were no other cars like it, Chrisman made single exhibition runs at tracks in SoCal and NorCal.

The drag race fans' response was overwhelming; they clamored for more cars like the Sachs and Sons Comet. The big three auto makers saw what was taking place at drag strips, and soon factory-backed clones of the Chrisman Comet began racing out of Michigan, Texas, and Illinois, and even a two-car team, "the Dodge Chargers," was touring the United States in late 1964. Almost overnight, blown and injected nitro-burning stock-bodied cars peppered the country, and track managers were cashing in on the new craze in drag racing. So, what was the name of this new class of drag car that every spectator wanted to see? To look at some of the cars entering this class, they appeared rather strange with their altered wheelbases, blowers, and injector stacks sticking out of the hood. Many names were used to describe this new breed of drag car, but the one that stuck was "funny car."

One of the first to make the leap into NorCal's funny car class was San Jose's Lew Arrington, who debuted his all-new "Brutus" Pontiac GTO in late 1965. Goodies Speed Shop employee Jim Liberman was at the controls of the nitro-burning GTO. A little-known fact about Brutus was that the design and lettering were done by Bobbie Liberman, Jim Liberman's new bride. Of course, Brutus was the first funny car sponsored by Richard Guess and his Goodies Speed Shop.

Seeing dollar signs in match racing a funny car, Joe Davis traded his Fiat body for a Mustang body. The Mustang body was fitted to his former altered chassis, and a blown nitro-burning Chevy engine replaced the blown gas-powered engine. Davis painted his new funny car and named it "Colt .45." He also debuted his Mustang in 1965 at Fremont, California. Davis, like Arrington, was based in San Jose.

In 1966, Jim Liberman was doing double duty by driving Lew Arrington's Brutus GTO and the Zucovich and Liberman "Hercules" injected nitro-burning Chevy Nova. The Hercules partnership was only temporary until Liberman finished his own blown nitro-burning Chevy Nova in late 1966. It was another funny car sponsored by Liberman's employer, Goodies Speed Shop in San Jose.

Driver Cecil Yother models the very latest in safety gear available in 1965. Fire was the main hazard for a driver in the very new funny car class. Having the best fire suit was critical for the driver's health and well-being. Yother had just taken over the "Melrose Missile" Mopar from Tommy Grove because Grove had made a great deal with Ford to become one of its factory funny car racers. Yother continued to maintain and drive the Melrose Missile into 1968.

NorCal's Dave Dozier wanted to cash in on the funny car fad by putting a 'Cuda body on his injected Hemi-powered dragster. His "Kop Kar" 'Cuda had high gear only and was hopelessly outclassed by funny cars of the day. Dave and his Kop Kar faded quickly in 1966.

With the help of Goodies Speed Shop owner Richard Guess, Rich Abate's "Samson" debuted in 1966. The car's first outings had an injected nitro-burning Hemi in the engine compartment, and Rich Hammons was the driver on its maiden runs. Hammons was also the full-time driver for the Hammons, Williamson, and Hammons Hairy Canary funny car. A big bad blown Hemi soon replaced the injected Hemi in the mighty Samson.

The closing months of 1966 saw Jim Liberman bring out his first Chevy Nova funny car. Again, it was sponsored by Goodies Speed Shop, Liberman's employer. Even though Liberman now had his own funny car, he continued to drive the Brutus GTO well into 1967. Late in 1967, Lew Arrington took over the driving duties of his Brutus GTO funny car, leaving Liberman to drive full-time in his own car.

Yet another car to debut in 1966 was the Hairy Canary of Hammons, Williamson, and Hammons, and it too was running under the Goodies Speed Shop banner. Rich Hammons drove "the Big Yellow Bird" while Don Williamson tuned the blown nitro-powered Hemi. The owners found out very quickly that having the engine in the stock position made the car very ill-handling and an adventure to drive for Rich Hammons. The Canary was revamped in 1967, moving the engine back under the windshield, which gave the car a better balance.

So how did this type of race car earn the name "funny car?" To answer this question, all one had to do is see how the once stock-bodied Melrose Missile was modified to become a funny car. The wheelbase was greatly altered, there was a fiberglass front clip, and fiberglass doors and a trunk lid were added. A roll cage was installed for driver safety, along with Plexiglas windows. Then there is the rather large injected Hemi sitting in the engine compartment. All this was around 1966 and was just the beginning of the funny car era.

Joe Davis and his Colt .45 Mustang squared off with "Dandy" Dick Landy at the 1966 *Hot Rod* magazine championship race at Riverside, California. Joe only raced one full season in his Colt .45 Mustang because of an incident in SoCal where he went into a tail-dragging wheel stand at 180 miles per hour. He successfully brought the sky-bound Mustang back to earth, but Davis was very shaken up after his flight at the finish line. That incident ended his funny car career, and he went altered racing with his longtime friend Wes Ingram in 1967.

The number-one sponsor for funny cars in NorCal was Richard Guess and his Goodies Speed Shop in San Jose, California. Guess had his speed shop logo on the Brutus GTO, Samson, the Hairy Canary, and Jim Liberman's Nova. Goodies Speed Shop became so popular in Northern California that Guess opened two more Goodies Speed Shops: one in Salinas and the other in San Bruno, California.

Entering the NorCal funny car fray in 1967 was the Campbell, California–based Parts Mart Camaro of Snell, Von Uhlit, and Burnett. The car was driven by Parts Mart owner Kip Brundage. The chassis and body were built by NorCal top fuel racer Frank Martinez and featured a big-block Chevy engine injected on nitro. By the end of 1967, Kip Brundage was the sole owner of the Camaro, and in 1968, a blower graced the Chevy engine.

Now for something different: a 1955 Chevrolet nitro-burning funny car named "Blown Hell" was the brainchild of San Jose racer Ron Rinauro, who introduced his 1955 Chevy to the world in 1967. The Shoebox featured a Ted Gotelli blown top fuel 392 Hemi—on nitro, of course. It was a big fan favorite when it raced, but the Gotelli-built 392 Hemi was very hard on transmission and driveline parts. It seemed that at every outing, Rinauro's racer spent more time in the pits than on the drag strip.

By 1967, Lew Arrington's Brutus GTO was much sleeker and aerodynamic. Jim Liberman was still driving with the engine lower and set back in the car because it handled better for Liberman. Its bright-orange color scheme became a Brutus trademark. Orange graced every single future Brutus funny car. Arrington's Brutus was getting noticed nationwide, and so were Liberman's driving skills.

NorCal's Ed Carter and Bob Little put the "fun" in funny car racing when they purchased the very used Blairs Speed Shop Nova from SoCal's Steve Bovan. The duo wasted no time refurbishing the tired Nova and renamed it the "Chevy II Heavy." Since both Carter and Little had real jobs, they raced mainly in NorCal and SoCal on weekends in 1967 and 1968. Their funny car was very outdated for its time, but they did not care—they just wanted to have fun.

Oakland's Romeo Palamides jumped on the funny car bandwagon with his jet engine–powered "Char Jet" Dodge Charger funny car. Romeo took a 1967 Dodge Charger and squeezed a J-34 jet engine into the all-steel stock-bodied car. He added a roll cage and race tires, making it a jet funny car ready to race. Ray Maurel was the chosen pilot for Romeo's Charger funny car. This was Romeo's 1967 version of a jet funny car; his 1968 version was named the "California Kid" with Don Beeman driving. It also had a Dodger Charger body.

In 1966, the Hairy Canary was one of those ill-handling funny cars that was an adventure in driving for driver Rich Hammons. To fix that problem, the engine was dropped down and moved back in 1967. This helped balance the car so the car would not scare Hammons or the spectators in the grandstands. Then, in 1968, Don Williamson became the full owner of the Big Yellow Bird as well as tuner and driver.

The Perry brothers' Orion Ford Mustang was a very strange combination of a Mustang body and a Pontiac engine. Early runs on the car were very scary for driver Paul Perry. After spinning the car out a few times, it was agreed a new driver was needed to solve the problem. The Perrys approached gas coupe driver Steve Woods to fill the driver's seat. Woods showed his driving skills by getting the ill-handling car to behave on its journey down the drag strip.

Coming out of the gas coupe class was the Hayward-based team of the Souza Bros. and Dad. Brother Harold built and tuned the Ford engine, while brother Dave drove their family-owned Ford Mustang funny car. Prior to their funny car, the Souzas raced a 1933 Willys coupe, and it was very popular with Bay Area race fans. The Souzas kept their Willys and, from time to time, brought it out and raced it at local drag strips. They also were guys with regular jobs, so they raced close to home and never left NorCal to race.

Late in 1967, Lew Arrington was driving his Brutus GTO funny car and experienced a horrific transmission explosion at Lions Drag Strip in SoCal. With the transmission in a million pieces and the fire out, Arrington crawled out of his race car without a scratch. The first thing Lew did was go over to starter Larry Sutton and thank him for insisting that he wear gloves. Arrington never wore gloves when he drove, but Sutton had insisted he wear gloves or he would not be able to make his run. Lew borrowed a pair of gloves, and the rest is history.

Beautiful was the only way to describe the "Lime Fire" 'Cuda funny car. This show-and-go race car sported a custom candy lime paint job and green-tinted Plexiglas windows. Felton, California, resident Jack Groner was the money man behind Lime Fire, and Clare Sanders was at the controls of the St. Clair–tuned Hemi-powered 'Cuda. For three years, Lime Fire raced in California and nearby states. Unfortunately, the car met with a sad end when it was parted out after those three seasons. The beautiful body ended up in a Florida swap meet some years later.

Oakland's Tommy Grove raced a Ford factory-backed funny car from 1966 to 1973. In this photograph, he is raising havoc at a funny car event in Puyallup, Washington. The Washington State spectators hated Grove and his Ford Mustang that evening because he was beating all the local favorites with his injected SOHC Ford-powered Mustang. The fans got so rowdy that the races had to be stopped twice to clean up beer bottles and cans that were thrown on the track. The fans were even throwing bottles and cans at Grove as he ran down the drag strip.

In 1967, NorCal's Butch Leal had the quickest and fastest nitro-burning injected funny car on planet earth. The Tulare-based Leal's "California Flash" 'Cuda toured the United States taking on any and all challengers. Leal wanted to stay with injectors as the big switch to blowers was taking place in the funny car world. Instead of switching, he quit funny car racing and went to super stock racing. He also went all out in his other passion: playing golf. Leal returned to drag racing in 1969 in the new pro stock class and became a superstar in the class.

Not a lot is known about the Garcia brothers and their "Out of Sight" Camaro funny car. The car debuted in late 1967 with Steve Garcia driving and brother Joe tuning the engine of the Sacramento-based team. The brothers raced mainly in NorCal in 1968. They also ventured to SoCal racetracks like Lions and Irwindale. Rumor has it that the brothers ran out of funds and parked their car at the end of 1968.

Fremont's John Skinner went from an owner and driver of a top gas dragster to his home-built "Man from Smoke" 'Cuda funny car. Skinner was looking for that pot of gold at the end of the funny car rainbow, but a high-gear-only 'Cuda did not generate much interest from promoters or track managers in NorCal. Unfortunately, the car was hopelessly outdated by the time Skinner brought it out to race.

These were new race cars for Lew Arrington and Jim Liberman in 1968. Gone was the GTO body on Arrington's Brutus; it was replaced with a sleek Pontiac Firebird body. A full funny car–style steel-tube chassis was installed under both Arrington's Firebird body and Liberman's Chevrolet Nova body. Arrington had a blown 392 Hemi for power, while Liberman went with a blown big-block Chevy engine, both on nitro, of course. These two racers were sponsored by Goodies Speed Shop out of San Jose, California, and were the best to represent NorCal in the growing funny car class.

The 1968 season saw Cecil Yother with an all-new-tube-chassis, fiberglass-flip-up-bodied Melrose Missile 'Cuda funny car. Like Butch Leal, Yother did not want to switch to a blown engine in the Missile. Since the big paychecks and bookings were now going to the blown funny car teams, everyone was switching to a blower. But not Leal or Yother; Cecil decided to quit funny car racing and devote his time to his very successful business, so the Missile was parked.

One of those injected cars that made the switch to a blower was Rich Abate's Samson, driven by Rich Hammons. Since Don Williamson now owned and drove the Hairy Canary, Hammons was the full-time driver for Samson. However, Abate's custom cabinet business took off, and Samson was left by the wayside in late 1968. Abate had no time to race Samson, so it was parked in favor of his business.

Another NorCal funny car that went the blower route was the Parts Mart Camaro of Kip Brundage. The year 1968 became the year of the blower in the funny car class. Here is Brundage testing his new blower set up at Fremont with no fire suit, no helmet, and an unknown setup that could have spelled disaster for Brundage. Thankfully, no problem occurred with the setup, and Brundage escaped his rather brainless stunt.

Oakland's Tommy Grove became North Carolina's Tommy Grove in 1968 when he bolted a blower on his 427 Ford SOHC engine and went on a nationwide tour with his Ford Mustang. Besides match racing, Grove also became a regular on the AHRA national event tour. Some years later, after he stopped racing, Grove became a major t-shirt manufacturer and multimillionaire in North Carolina.

The Watts brothers and their "Watts Riot" Camaro raced one very memorable time in 1968 at Fremont. The throttle stuck wide open as it was fired up, and with the rear tires smoking, it came flying out of the staging lanes striking the crowd control officer. Then it spun around and ran into the billboard signs behind the starting line. With the throttle still wide open, the car began to climb up the signs, stood on its tail, and finally ran out of fuel and shut off. The driver was not hurt, but the crowd control officer suffered two broken legs.

In February 1968, Jim Liberman took his Nova to Lions Drag Strip in Long Beach, California. There he won the largest funny car event ever held in the United States, cementing Liberman as one of the "must-have" race cars by drag strip promoters nationwide in 1968 and beyond. A bonus for promoters and track managers was Liberman's wild driving style of long smoke-filled burnouts. His wheels-up starting line launches really made him a fan favorite from coast to coast.

Russell James Liberman lived from September 12, 1945, to September 9, 1977, and was the ultimate showman in a funny car. He ran over 100 dates a year with his funny car. He was voted the 17th all-time driver by NHRA and the No. 1 funny car driver on the 50th anniversary of the funny car in 2019. That vote was taken among current funny car fans. Many had never seen Liberman race. However, they enjoyed the many stories of his exploits on and off the racetrack. To them, "Jungle Jim" Liberman still lives on.

The "Proud American" Corvette was Ed Carter's funny car venture in 1969 and 1970. The Newark-based Carter first raced with engines by ex-top fuel racer Del Doss. When that partnership soured, NorCal's Rich Guasco supplied a 392 Hemi for Carter's Corvette. However, it seemed like the Corvette curse plagued Carter like it did so many other funny car racers with Corvette bodies.

In 1969, NHRA started a new funny car eliminator class at its national events beginning with the NHRA Winternationals in Pomona, California. When the smoke and nitro fumes had cleared, Clare Sanders, driving his team "Jungle Jim" Nova, was in the Pomona winner's circle. This win had even more promoters wanting the Jungle Jim show at their racetrack for the 1969 season. Liberman went out and purchased Marc Susman's Nova funny car, and Susman became part of team Jungle Jim. The third car helped meet the promoters' demand for a Jungle Jim Nova at their racetrack.

This almost-new-and-improved Souza Bros. and Dad Ford Mustang was photographed in 1969. The car featured a longer front clip and a 427 Ford SOHC engine with a blower. But alas, by funny car standards, the car was outdated with no tube chassis or one-piece fiberglass body, making it too heavy to compete with the funny cars of the day in 1969.

Fresno's Ed Wills made a big change in 1971. He left behind his top fuel dragster for an all-new "Mr. Ed" Dodge Charger funny car with SoCal's Dave Beebe at the controls. Wills raced in the funny car class until 1973 with a Plymouth Satellite–bodied funny car. Some of the drivers who drove for Wills were Dave Beebe, Kelly Brown, Mike Snively, and Bobby Rowe. At the end of 1973, Wills sold his entire rig to Texas funny car racer Mike Burkhart and went back to top fuel racing.

Frustration and anger are the only words to describe NorCal funny car owner Rich Guasco's emotions as his "Pure Hell" funny car burned to the ground. This happened at Fremont in 1971 on Guasco's first funny car outing. Luckily, driver Elwyn "Honker" Carlson escaped the fiberglass inferno without a scratch. The car was a total loss, but Guasco returned later with a different car. (Courtesy of the Jamie Jackson/Mike Bagnod collection.)

Jungle Jim Liberman made the switch to a Chevrolet Camaro body in 1971. Also gone was the Goodies Speed Shop, and in its place was Honest Charley's Speed Shop. This was because he was based in West Chester, Pennsylvania, where he had moved. He picked up Briggs Chevrolet, based in South Amboy, New Jersey. Soon, Revell models made him an offer he could not refuse, and Jungle Jim became Revell's Jungle Jim.

Gary "Tango" Matranga gave the funny car class a try in 1971 with his "Day-Go Express" Camaro. At Sacramento, Gary's Camaro had a very nasty blower explosion off the starting line. Nobody was hurt, but Gary's wallet was emptied in the boomer. In 1972, he fielded an all-new Vega funny car, but success eluded Matranga. He left drag racing to build show-winning street rods. In the mid-1990s, he returned to drag racing for a short time with a retro front-engine fuel dragster. (Courtesy of the Jamie Jackson/Mike Bagnod collection.)

It was 1972, and musician John Kinsel's "the Drummer" Camaro was the only funny car in NorCal that was still racing with a fuel injected Hemi engine. There was no blower for Kinsel; his Camaro traveled to SoCal to race in the fuel injected funny car circuit. Kinsel and driver Lorry Azevedo traveled the year racing NHRA national events. At those events, the Drummer raced dragsters, gassers, and altereds in competition eliminator.

The Burkholder brothers parked their fuel altered and the Speigel brothers parked their supercharged gas coupe and combined forces in "the Brotherhood" funny car in 1972. It proved to be a very short partnership for the foursome. The car was driven by Harry Burkholder until the end of 1972, then all parties decided to retire from drag racing altogether. The main reason was to spend more time with their families.

The San Jose–based Motta and Williamson "Hairy Canary II" was truly a rare car in the funny car class. It was one of a few rear-engine funny cars trying to compete in the class in 1972. Dave Motta drove and Don Williamson tuned the bright-yellow Dodge Challenger–bodied funny car. A lack of sponsorship and funds forever parked this funny car.

The second time was the charm for Rich Guasco and his Pure Hell funny car. After his first car burned to the ground in 1971, Guasco returned in 1972 with an all-new "Pure Hell" Demon-bodied funny car. This time, SoCal's Dave Beebe was at the controls of Guasco's Dodge Demon. The following year at the NHRA Springnationals in Columbus, Ohio, Guasco and Beebe won funny car eliminator. But the Pure Hell body had been replaced with Larry Huff's "Soapy Sales" Challenger body, making it the team of Larry Huff, Rich Guasco, and Dave Beebe as the winner.

After a series of gas coupes and a Corvette roadster, San Francisco's Mike Mitchell went big time in 1972, debuting his all-new "Hippie" 'Cuda funny car. It was a real piece of rolling art in the funny car class. Unfortunately, it did not run as well as it looked, and two bad fires wore it out in 1972 and 1973. Mitchell retired at the end of 1973 but returned briefly in 1980 with a Corvette funny car. However, the Corvette curse struck again when he crashed his almost new car in mid-1980 and retired for good.

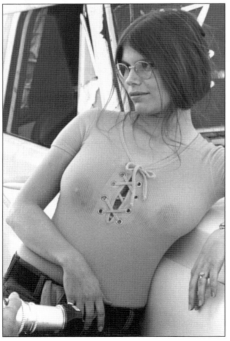

In the early 1970s, every adolescent male drag fan's dream girl was Jungle Jim Liberman's girlfriend and pit crew Pam Hardy, also known as "Jungle Pam." Pam poured the bleach for burnouts, backed the car up, and helped Liberman stage the car. She also checked under the car for water or oil leakage. The fans loved her gyrations out on the racetrack, and promoters paid extra to have her do her thing with Jungle Jim's race car at their racetrack.

Jungle Jim Liberman switched to a Chevy Monza–bodied funny car in 1977. This marked his 12th year driving in the funny car class. In those years, it is estimated Liberman owned and sold over 35 funny cars. At times, he had three to four team Jungle funny cars running all over the United States at one time. Sadly, Liberman died on September 9, 1977, in a highway accident in West Chester, Pennsylvania, while driving his Corvette. He was only 31 years old, but his legacy lives on to this day.

For a short stint, Dick Oswald and Dave Uyehara went funny car racing with their "Kamikaze" Monza funny car. It was short-lived because of a stuck throttle at the NHRA Winternationals in Pomona, California. This resulted in a two-car get-together, destroying their Kamikaze and Ron Correnti's new Ford Thunderbird funny car. Neither driver was injured in the accident. Correnti returned to drive another funny car, but Oswald and Uyehara retired.

Former drag boat racer Ron Williams went funny car racing in 1972 with his "Shakey" Ford Pinto–bodied funny car. Out of all the funny car owners that came out of NorCal, Williams was still racing funny cars well into the 1980s. His cars were all named "Shakey," and they consisted of a Ford Pinto, Dodge Charger, Ford Mustang II, and Corvette. At one point, Williams was the only funny car owner/driver left in NorCal.

Based in Tulare, California, was the team of Steve Rohn and Louis Sweet. The "Instant Nut" was their Monza-bodied funny car. Their funny car doubled as a fuel altered—when the team wanted to race in a fuel altered show, they just switched bodies. Louis Sweet drove the car when it was a fuel altered, and Steve Rohn drove when it was a funny car.

NorCal's Bill Hoge was a movie stunt driver and an owner/driver of his "Willie and the Poor Boys" Dodge Omni funny car. He purchased his Omni with the money he earned doing stunt work for the movie *More American Graffiti*. He also made enough money to get a trailer for Willie and the Poor Boys. Proving funny car owners will take any sponsor they can get, Hoge was sponsored by the Boys Club of Fremont, California.

Four

LITTLE GUYS

BACKBONE OF THE SPORT

Since the beginning of drag racing in Northern California, the little guy racer was the main supporter of racetracks. Without the stock cars, gas coupes, roadsters, and altereds, the drag strips could not have survived. Sure, dragsters, nitro and gas, helped put people in the grandstands. Then the funny car fad came about and helped the spectator count also. However, the little guy racer entry fees paid the bills for a drag strip to function. Many of those so-called little guy racers used their first race car as a stepping stone to be able to move up into a more powerful and faster race car. Drag racing will always be a family sport with entire families participating in building and racing their car.

Unfortunately, time has not been kind to NorCal drag racers. At one time, over 17 drag strips ran almost full-time throughout the year. But sadly, one by one, their doors closed forever, with at last count only six remaining open. Of those six, only four have any sort of regular race dates. Long gone are the weekly and monthly shows that flourished in the 1960s and early 1970s. In NorCal, the sport of drag racing will never be what it once was, and that is very sad. Gone are most of the speed shops, chassis builders, custom painters, and craftsmen that made the sport great in Northern California. Only a few still remain as a reminder of those glory days of Northern California drag racing.

Northern California individuals that have earned a coveted membership in the International Drag Racing Hall of Fame are as follows: Gary Ormsby, Frank Bradley, Don Cook, and Tony Waters (top fuel owners/drivers), James Warren, Roger Coburn, and Marvin Miller (top fuel team), Rich Guasco and Dale Emery (fuel altered team), Romeo Palamides and Bob Smith (jet car team), Jim McLennen (racer and track manager), Dave Uyehara (driver and chassis builder), Kent Fuller (chassis builder), Butch Leal (pro stock driver/owner), Jim Liberman (funny car owner/driver), Shirley Shahan (pioneer woman racer), and Steve Reyes (action photographer).

In 1963, Fred Sorensen was part of the team of Argee, Sorensen, and Burkholder. They set the standard 1,320 record of 170.77 miles per hour for fuel roadsters and won No. 3 eliminator at the 1963 Bakersfield March Meet. This is Fred Sorensen racing his own fuel roadster, with Jim Herbert at the controls, in 1965. Sorensen's fuel roadster was a NorCal fan favorite wherever it raced because of its lumbering smoke-filled quarter-mile runs.

Top fuel dragster owner/driver Rich Guasco wanted to race something different after selling his dragster to San Francisco's Chuck Flores. So Guasco had Pete Ogden build the chassis for an all-new fuel altered, creating Pure Hell in 1964. Fred Cerutti was the shakedown driver for the new bantam-bodied altered. After the shakedown runs were completed, Tony Del Rio did the custom paint job. Then the Pleasanton-based Guasco put Don "the Golden Shoe" Petrich behind the steering wheel. The duo quickly started to smash track records and win altered races in both Northern and Southern California.

Sixty-five-year-old Walt Ross felt age was just a number as he raced his nitro-burning Harley Davidson throughout NorCal in 1965. Ross set records at every track he ran in the mid-1960s. He even ventured to the Bonneville salt flats to run his Harley as a land-speed bike. Walt proved that going fast makes one young at heart.

Roger Hardcastle's "Stinger II" was something way different in 1965. His sporty hand-built Stinger II was a one-of-a-kind race car. The car ran a blown 392 Hemi on pump gasoline and had loads of power. Maybe it was too much power, because his "Stinger I" flew at the finish line at Cotati, California, destroying itself upon landing. Roger walked away from the wreckage unhurt and quickly began rebuilding his crunched race car.

Dixon, California's Fred Sorensen debuted a revamped fuel roadster for 1966. The car was completely redone and even featured a new/old driver in former partner Don Argee. Argee split driving time between his top fuel dragster and Fred's roadster. When he was not driving a race car, Argee drove a cement truck for a living in Sacramento.

Shirley Shahan helped to open a lot of doors for female drag racers in the mid-1960s. The Tulare, California–based Shahan was a proven star in the super stock classes with her "Drag-on Lady" Mopar. Her notable accomplishments caught the attention of AMC executives, and she soon became an AMC factory-backed racer from 1968 to 1971. Racing was not her only interest; she was also a star softball player, a power company executive, and a full-time wife and mother.

NorCal seemed to be the land of the different race cars, and San Jose's Terry Davis led the pack. Davis raced a very different style of altered, as it was an enclosed bantam-bodied race car. His "Vulture" sat high enough that the rollbar and Davis's head stuck out the roof of the body. This was the first of five different altereds that Davis raced in NorCal between 1966 and 1970. Then in 1971, Davis debuted a slingshot-style twin-engine dragster.

In the mid-1960s, when NHRA approved fiberglass bodies for altereds, Pete and Harry Burkholder discarded their all-steel Fiat body for a lightweight bantam body. The Sacramento-based brothers ran a blown Oldsmobile engine in their altered. The car ran great and looked good enough to appear on the August 1966 cover of *Drag Racing* magazine. It was one of the first NorCal race cars to achieve that honor.

San Jose's John L. Williams was an auto mechanic during the week, and on weekends, he could be found drag racing his "Fugitive" at NorCal drag strips in 1966. Williams removed his Simca body for a lightweight fiberglass bantam body. With Goodies Speed Shop as his main sponsor, Williams terrorized the altered ranks for the next seven-plus seasons.

The Battle of the Bay Area gas coupes was between Hambaris and Mitchell and the Warren brothers and Miller. The 1967 battle was won by the San Francisco–based Hambaris and Mitchell, driven by Mike Mitchell. Mitchell soon became the sole owner of the 1933 Willys. Later, he sold the car and built a Corvette roadster. Then he made the jump to the funny car class with a 'Cuda funny car. The Warren brothers and Miller Willys was then sold and became the Del Rio and Carlson "Blue Dog" gas coupe.

Putting on a show for gas coupe fans were the Brasher and Cummings "BC" 1933 Willys and the Schuck, Eplin, and Schuck 1948 Anglia. Both were regulars at NorCal drag strips in 1967. When 1968 dawned, the Brasher and Cummings Willys had a new look, with a color change to purple. The biggest change was to the engine compartment; gone was the injected Chevy, and in its place was a blown Chevy engine.

"Charlie's Business Coupe" was a fun car to watch run with driver Slim Summer making smoke-filled passes every time it ran. This car was unique because of the 1934 Ford body mounted on the dragster frame. There really was not a class for the car to compete, so it ended up with all different kinds of dragsters and altereds that had clocked the same quarter-mile times. The other special thing about this car is that it still exists today and is race-ready.

San Jose's Goodknight, Keith, and Williamson were NorCal's "rock stars" in the top gas dragster class. In 1964, the trio was handpicked to be on the first US drag team to visit England. Driver Bob Keith made drag racing history when he drove the first American dragster to ever make a run on UK soil. The team returned to the United States and competed in top gas until the class ended in 1971.

In 1967 and 1968, the team of Halstead and Dunlap ran in both top fuel and top gas. For a short time in 1968, the San Jose–based duo ran a Ford 427 SOHC engine in their dragster. They ran the Ford engine in top fuel and top gas, and their car was the only dragster to run this type of engine in top fuel and top gas in NorCal.

Pairing a blown nitro-burning roadster against a twin-engine dragster is something that happened on a regular basis in NorCal. Castro Valley's Fred Cerutti was the owner/driver of the "Quality Auto" fuel altered, and Newark's Leo Dunn was the owner/driver of the twin-engine dragster. Both gentlemen were longtime NorCal drag racers and big fan favorites wherever they raced in Northern California.

A great example of "little guy" racers was an AMC Rambler versus a Chevrolet Corvette. The Oakland AMC dealership of Roberts Rambler promoted AMC products by racing on a weekly basis at NorCal drag strips. These door-slammer stock-style cars were what paid the bills for a drag strip to open its doors. Their entry fee paid for insurance, track workers, and general repairs to the track; without these racers' support, a track could not exist.

San Jose's Courtesy Chevrolet sponsored two popular race cars that attended NorCal drag strips. This was its Super Stock Camaro; the other car was a top gas dragster. Both were maintained and driven by Ron Love, a Courtesy employee. The Camaro was a four-wheel rolling billboard for the dealership.

Hayward's Ron Nunes had one of the few blown gas coupes in NorCal. His 1941 Willys "Glass Spook" was also a weekend regular at NorCal drag strips. Whenever Nunes was not flying high in his gas coupe, he could be found at his day job as a sheet metal fabricator.

Here is a NorCal odd couple: Lee Loretz and his "Lee's T" running against Rob Stirling driving his injected nitro-burning dragster. When Loretz was not doing battle on the racetrack, he could be found in his TV sales and repair shop in Hayward. Stirling was based in Salinas and worked part-time at his dad's auto repair shop. Loretz retired his Lee's T after a few seasons of racing; however, Stirling kept racing well into the 1970s. Stirling went top fuel racing with a rear-engine Chevy-powered dragster.

It seemed like the Bay Area–based Steve Woods always tried something different to conquer the quarter-mile. His blown Hemi-powered winged Anglia was about as different as he could get in 1967. The Anglia was neither a funny car nor a dragster; it was a one-of-a-kind race car that was so much fun to watch run. Woods was very exciting to watch drive his nitro-powered Anglia as he tried to get it down the drag strip. The car had a mind of its own, and Woods made half-mile runs down the quarter-mile racetrack very exciting.

NorCal drag racers recycled even back in 1967. Denny Martinez fulfilled a lifelong dream to own and drive a fuel altered when he purchased the first "Pure Heaven" fuel altered from SoCal's Leon Fitzgerald. Martinez had a great time running his newly named "Blue Max" fuel altered at NorCal drag strips. Alas, Martinez's racer consumed parts and money, and he was forced to park his dream race car forever.

Dixon, California, resident Fred Sorensen debuted his all-new wild and woolly "Warlock" fuel altered in 1967 with Herb Pickney driving. To say this car was a fan favorite was a gross understatement. The Warlock lived up to its name because it was evil handling, and driver Herb Pickney worked hard to get the car to the finish line at any track.

This proud gentleman was Leroy Philson with his "Mighty Mouse" 1956 Chevy gasser. Leroy was one of the few black racers in NorCal around 1967. His wife, Bonny, also drove and raced their 1941 Willys truck. If there was a drag race happening in NorCal, this husband-and-wife team was there having a great time.

Another well-known race car from NorCal was the Davis and Ingram Jewel T, a blown gas-burning altered. Wes Ingram (left) and Joe Davis (right) combined resources and came up with a true show-and-go race car. Their first year together was in 1967, when the San Jose–based duo set many track records and drew national attention when the car appeared on the cover of the October 1967 issue of *All American Drags* magazine.

The top gas dragster team of Airigoni and Grigg had one of those bad days at Vacaville in 1967. Driver Glen Grigg survived a horrific fire and crash at the finish line. Grigg was banged up and broke a leg, but the team rebuilt to race again. With Grigg on the mend, Frankie Silva took over driving duties until Grigg could return.

Sacramento's Gary Matranga had the very dubious honor that no dragster driver wanted, crashing two cars in one day. In 1968, Matranga managed to crash Jim Guy's top gas dragster (pictured) and then hopped into the Cheetah II top fuel dragster and crashed it. Both crashes happened at Fremont. Guy rebuilt his dragster, and Matranga continued to drive for him, but the Cheetah II was replaced, with Johnny Cox driving.

Johnny Austin, from Richmond, California, was one of those little guy top gas dragster owners/ drivers who was a weekend warrior at local NorCal drag strips. Austin's real job was as a machinist at UC Berkley during the week. He also built small water pumps for dragsters in his spare time. When he was not racing his car, he could be found helping top fuel racer Roger Harrington, who was also based in the Richmond area.

Ron Robles and Pat Brosnan made NorCal proud with their "Norm's Barber Shop" Nova. The Livermore-based team went to the 1968 NHRA Winternationals, held in Pomona, California, and took home top stock eliminator honors. The little Nova waded through some of the finest stock cars in the country for the victory.

The Del Rio brothers—Tony, Wayne, and Chris—were big supporters of NorCal drag racing. They owned a gas station/auto shop in San Lorenzo. Out of their shop, they raced two gas coupes, one an Anglia (far side) and one a 1933 Willys (near side). Tony was also a custom painter who had painted Rich Guasco's Pure Hell fuel altered and the Hay and Walsh Wailer top fuel dragster, just to name a few. Whenever an out-of-town racer needed a place to work on their car, the Del Rios opened their shop to all that needed a hand 24 hours a day.

NorCal did not have a lot of super stock racers but filling that void was Harry Holton and his "Hemi Countdown" Mopar. Holton and his mighty Mopar raced all over NorCal and ventured to SoCal for any large NHRA national events. Harry also raced at AHRA national events and, in 1967, was the AHRA super stock world champion.

In the late 1960s, NorCal's "Panella Trucking" Anglia gas coupe was a very popular race car. Driver Ken Dondero amazed race fans with his driving ability as he drove the short-wheel-base car while shifting the four-speed transmission. The little candy apple red Anglia pulled the front wheels up each time Dondero shifted. When Panella retired the Anglia, Dondero became a much sought-after journeyman pro stock driver. He drove for Don Nicholson and Gapp and Roush, to name a few.

It was something other fuel altered racers did not want to see in 1968. NorCal's Rich Guasco went from a blown Chevrolet engine to a big bad blown 392 Hemi in his Pure Hell fuel altered. Driver Dale "the Snail" Emery was able to crank out 200-mile-per-hour runs on a regular basis and put other fuel altereds on the trailer in 1968 and 1969.

Honda motorcycle owners had something to cheer about at NorCal drag strips in 1968. Rich (left) and Donny Ornellas (right) had the quickest and fastest Honda-powered drag bikes in the country. Brother Rich tuned the nitro-burning Honda engine and Brother Donny rode their one-of-a-kind home-built drag bike. This bike is still around today, and it has been restored to its glory days of racing.

Proving that drag racers will take what they can as a sponsorship, Buzzy Wadsworth delighted NorCal male race fans with his "Booby Hatch" sponsorship of his injected Chevy bantam altered. The Booby Hatch was a Newark-based topless dancer and beer bar that was very similar to San Francisco's North Beach topless dancer clubs in 1967–1968.

The only factory-backed black racer in NorCal was Richmond's Corky Booze (pronounced "Boo-say"). AMC provided Booze with his AMX Javelin, and he did not let AMC down. He could be seen all over NorCal racing his "Charlie Brown" Javelin. When he was not racing, Corky was an auto shop teacher, and later, he became a city council member of Richmond. Before the Javelin, Corky and his brother Virian raced a 1955 Chevrolet gasser. The brothers were well-known racers at all NorCal drag strips.

Castro Valley's Fred Cerutti was one diehard fuel altered owner/driver. Cerutti parked his outdated fuel altered for an all-new Quality Auto Bantam fuel altered in 1969. Fred made the five-hour tow each way from his shop in Castro Valley to SoCal to race at fuel altered events each weekend. NorCal had no real fuel altered events for Cerutti to race in 1969, so he went where the races were.

Sacramento's Harry and Pete Burkholder were longtime fuel altered racers. They started in 1961 and ran altered classes until 1972, when they raced briefly in the funny car class. The car shown here was a one-of-a-kind altered built by the Burkholders. The brothers combined two 1923 T fiberglass bodies to make one 1923 Touring body. In 1970, the brothers took their Touring-bodied fuel altered to Bakersfield and won fuel altered eliminator over the best cars in the country. Pete and Harry Burkholder considered that win the biggest of their racing careers.

Quite a few NorCal drag teams consisted of bands of brothers. Here, the Trillo brothers' "Judge" altered took on the Boudakian brothers' altered at Bakersfield, California. Both cars were blown gas altereds and raced primarily in NorCal. Jimmy Trillo drove the Judge, which was based in San Jose. Harry, Charlie, and Jack Boudakian were based in Visalia, California. The altered class was a stepping stone for Trillos, as they soon fielded a top fuel dragster. The Boudakian brothers updated their blown gas altered for future NorCal races.

Hayward's Ed Terry was one of two factory Ford-sponsored racers in NorCal. While the other Ford-backed racer (Tommy Grove) went into the funny car class, Terry stayed with the door slammer classes. Terry did very well for Ford, so in 1970, he was rewarded, becoming a Ford-backed pro stock racer. As a Ford Maverick pro stock racer, Terry became part of a nationwide effort by Ford in drag racing. However, by the end of 1970, Ford changed its direction and withdrew from drag racing. This left Terry and other factory-backed racers without a sponsorship for 1971.

A very grim day in the life of NorCal's Terry Erven was on July 29, 1962. Erven was one half of a two-car dragster crash that killed Texas racer Douglas Royal at Fremont drag strip. Erven suffered very serious injuries and burns when his engine came back and landed on him. Erven finally recovered enough to return to drag racing in 1965. He raced several dragsters and one other fuel altered before his Axis Power fuel altered in 1970.

Sacramento's Nick Otto made Fred Sorensen a deal he could not refuse and purchased the Warlock fuel altered in 1970. Frank Pitts sold his top fuel dragster and became a partner/driver in the Warlock with Otto. But things did not work out for the partners, as a huge explosion and fire caused Pitts to lose control of the Warlock at the Sacramento finish line. The car veered off the track and into a culvert and destroyed itself on impact. Pitts lived through the crash but came out a quadriplegic. Otto did not rebuild the Warlock.

The Del Rio brothers are seen here in 1971 with their all-new street roadster. This was not any ordinary race car but the winner of the 1971 Grand National Oakland roadster show's Most Beautiful Roadster. To start the 1971 racing season, the Del Rios took their roadster to the NHRA Winternationals in Pomona, California. At this event, they won best appearing car, and in 1971, the car graced the covers of several car magazines. Fifty years after its debut, the car is still in the Del Rio family and races at nostalgia events in NorCal with Eric Reyes driving.

Friends and foes battled at the NHRA US Nationals in Indiana. Neighbors from Tulare, California, Butch Leal and Shirley Shahan went toe-to-toe in their factory-backed Pro Stock racers, Leal in his California Flash Mopar and Shahan in her Drag-on Lady AMC Hornet. Leal won the battle of Tulare neighbors on this long-ago day. Leal continued racing for Mopar, but Shahan lost her factory backing at the end of 1971 when AMC quit racing.

The dawn of a new class of drag racing came about in 1979. The Sacramento-based Dave Riolo and his Chevrolet "Temptation" led the charge on the West Coast for a new class of drag racing, the pro modified (or "pro mod"). On the East Coast, Charles Carpenter and his 1955 Chevrolet also laid claim to starting the new pro mod class. To this day, fans of the class will argue who owned and drove the first pro mod race car. Of course, California fans back Riolo, and North Carolina fans back Carpenter.

Another brother team in NorCal was the Reineros, out of Merced. Brother Gary drove their Willys gasser, and after the Willys was retired, a 1948 Austin gas coupe took over. The Reineros could be found racing anywhere and everywhere in NorCal in the late 1960s and 1970s.

In the mid-1980s, Tulare-based Louis Sweet's "Sweet Thrills" fuel altered was the last of its kind in NorCal. Sweet drove his fuel altered, making him the world's quickest, fastest pharmacist. Soon, the roadster body was removed for a Chevy Monza body. The Sweet Thrills fuel altered became the Instant Nut funny car with the body change. The car also had a driver change: Steve Rohn drove when it was a funny car, and Sweet drove when it was a fuel altered.

DISCOVER THOUSANDS OF LOCAL HISTORY BOOKS FEATURING MILLIONS OF VINTAGE IMAGES

Arcadia Publishing, the leading local history publisher in the United States, is committed to making history accessible and meaningful through publishing books that celebrate and preserve the heritage of America's people and places.

Find more books like this at
www.arcadiapublishing.com

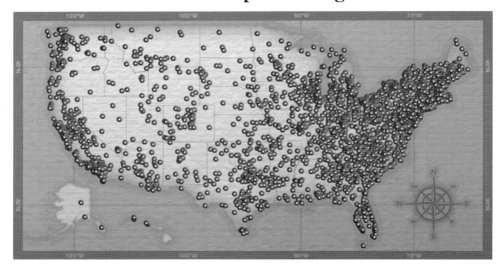

Search for your hometown history, your old stomping grounds, and even your favorite sports team.

Consistent with our mission to preserve history on a local level, this book was printed in South Carolina on American-made paper and manufactured entirely in the United States. Products carrying the accredited Forest Stewardship Council (FSC) label are printed on 100 percent FSC-certified paper.

MADE IN THE USA